WHO EATS WHAT?
FOREST FOOD CHAINS

by Rebecca Pettiford

Ideas for Parents and Teachers

Pogo Books let children practice reading informational text while introducing them to nonfiction features such as headings, labels, sidebars, maps, and diagrams, as well as a table of contents, glossary, and index.

Carefully leveled text with a strong photo match offers early fluent readers the support they need to succeed.

Before Reading

- "Walk" through the book and point out the various nonfiction features. Ask the student what purpose each feature serves.

- Look at the glossary together. Read and discuss the words.

Read the Book

- Have the child read the book independently.

- Invite him or her to list questions that arise from reading.

After Reading

- Discuss the child's questions. Talk about how he or she might find answers to those questions.

- Prompt the child to think more. Ask: What other forest animals and plants do you know about? What food chains do you think they are a part of?

Pogo Books are published by Jump!
5357 Penn Avenue South
Minneapolis, MN 55419
www.jumplibrary.com

Library of Congress Cataloging-in-Publication Data

Names: Pettiford, Rebecca, author.
Pettiford, Rebecca. Who eats what?
Title: Forest food chains / by Rebecca Pettiford.
Description: Minneapolis, MN: Jump!, Inc. [2017]
Series: Who eats what? | "Pogo Books are published by Jump!" | Audience: Ages 7-10.
Identifiers: LCCN 2016028290 (print)
LCCN 2016029219 (ebook)
ISBN 9781620315743 (hardcover : alk. paper)
ISBN 9781620316139 (pbk.)
ISBN 9781624965227 (ebook)
Subjects: LCSH: Forest ecology–Juvenile literature.
Food chains (Ecology)–Juvenile literature.
Classification: LCC QH541.5.F6 P4485 2017 (print)
LCC QH541.5.F6 (ebook) | DDC 577.3–dc23
LC record available at https://lccn.loc.gov/2016028290

Editor: Jenny Fretland VanVoorst
Book Designer: Michelle Sonnek
Photo Researcher: Michelle Sonnek

Photo Credits: All photos by Shutterstock except: age fotostock, 10-11, 20-21bm; Alamy, 19, 20-21t, 20-21tm, 20-21b; Getty, 9; iStock, 3, 6-7; Minden Pictures, 12-13.

Printed in the United States of America at Corporate Graphics in North Mankato, Minnesota.

TABLE OF CONTENTS

CHAPTER 1

FOREST ADAPTATIONS

The **deciduous** forest **biome** is home to many plants and animals. Summers are warm. Winters are cold.

In the fall, trees such as oaks and maples lose their leaves. Losing leaves is an **adaptation**. It helps trees survive the cold winter.

Forest animals adapt, too. Some **hibernate** in winter. They grow thick fur to keep warm.

Many birds move to warmer areas. They return in the spring.

Most insects lay their eggs before winter begins. They hatch in spring.

WHERE ARE THEY?

There are deciduous forests in the eastern part of North America, Europe, and Asia.

■ = Deciduous Forests

N
W — E
S

CHAPTER 2

THE FOREST FOOD CHAIN

Like all living things, forest plants and animals need energy to live and grow. Food is energy. Plants make their own food. Animals eat plants and other animals.

A **food chain** shows how energy moves from plants to animals. Each living link in the chain eats the one before it.

deer
(consumer)

tree
(producer)

In the forest, trees and mosses are **producers**. They use energy from the sun, soil, and water to make their own food. They are the first link in the food chain.

Deer and mice eat leaves and seeds. So do chipmunks and squirrels. They are **consumers**, the next link in the chain.

DID YOU KNOW?

Most animals eat more than one type of food. They belong to many different food chains. These food chains form a food web.

Animals such as coyotes and raccoons are **predators**. So are owls and snakes. They hunt and eat consumers. They are the next link in the food chain.

Large predators will eat smaller predators. For example, an owl will eat a snake.

vole
(consumer)

coyote
(predator)

fungi
(decomposers)

CHAPTER 2

When an animal or plant dies, **bacteria**, worms, and **fungi** break it down. They are **decomposers**, the last link in the chain.

Decomposers return **nutrients** to the soil. The nutrients help trees and other plants grow.

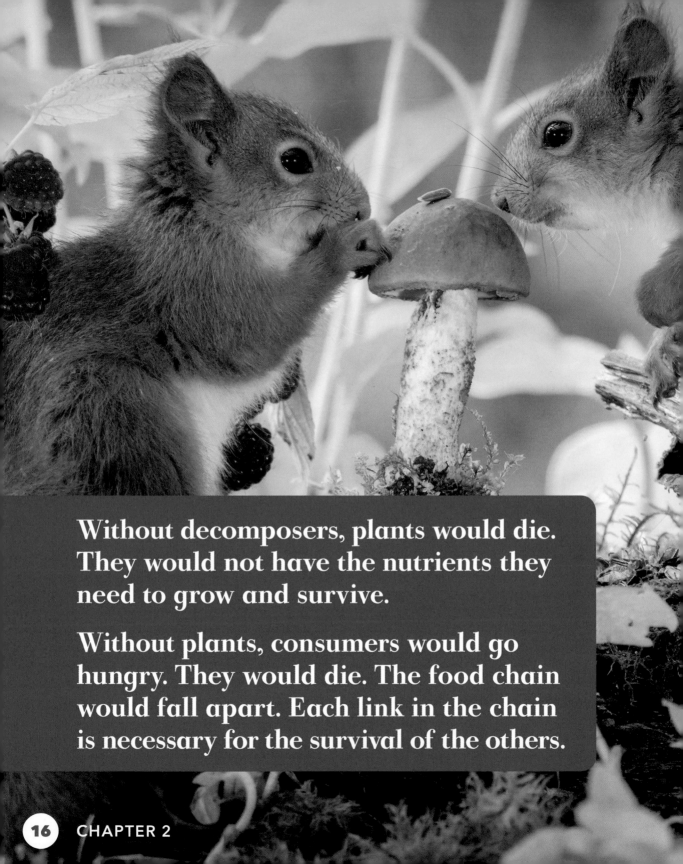

Without decomposers, plants would die. They would not have the nutrients they need to grow and survive.

Without plants, consumers would go hungry. They would die. The food chain would fall apart. Each link in the chain is necessary for the survival of the others.

TAKE A LOOK!

One forest food chain might look something like this:

Producer:
Fern

Predator:
Coyote

Consumer:
Deer

Decomposer:
Bacteria

CHAPTER 3

· ·

FOOD CHAIN CLOSE-UPS

Let's look at a simple food chain. Seeds fall from a forest tree. A pheasant eats them.

A bobcat eats the pheasant.
In time, the bobcat dies.
Bacteria break down its body.
The nutrients make the soil rich.
The food chain begins again.

Let's look at another food chain.

1) This one starts with seeds.

2) A mouse eats the seeds.

3) An owl eats the mouse.

4) Later, the owl dies. Worms break down its body. The nutrients help forest plants grow.

The food chain continues!

ACTIVITIES & TOOLS

THE FOREST IN YOUR NEIGHBORHOOD

A forest provides a home for plants and animals. No matter where you live, you are likely to have a tiny forest in your neighborhood. Grab a pencil and a notepad. Go to your local park or your backyard. You should find trees and wildlife. Do the following:

❶ Choose a tree to study. Look down around the tree for leaves, twigs, flowers, seeds, or fruits. Look up in the branches. Can you see and hear signs of life?

❷ List the plants that live on or make use of this tree.

❸ List the animals that live on or make use of this tree. Do not forget the insects!

❹ List the things that the tree gives these plants and animals.

❺ How is the tree like your own home? How is it different?

GLOSSARY

adaptation: A change that helps plants and animals survive the conditions of a natural area.

bacteria: Tiny life forms that break down dead animals.

biome: A large area on Earth defined by the weather, land, and type of plants and animals that live there.

consumers: Animals that eat plants.

deciduous: A tree or shrub that loses its leaves every year.

decomposers: Life forms that break down dead matter.

food chain: An ordering of plants and animals in which each uses or eats the one before it for energy.

fungi: Living things, such as molds and mushrooms, that have no leaves, flowers, or roots and live on plant or animal matter.

hibernate: Sleeping or resting through the winter.

nutrients: Substances that are essential for living things to survive and grow.

omnivores: Animals that eat plants and other animals.

predators: Animals that hunt and eat other animals.

producers: Plants that make their own food from the sun.

INDEX

TO LEARN MORE

Learning more is as easy as 1, 2, 3.

1) Go to www.factsurfer.com

2) Enter "forestfoodchains" into the search box.

3) Click the "Surf" button to see a list of websites.

With factsurfer, finding more information is just a click away.